The B.E.E. Kids

Put on Your Thinking H.O.T.S

Written and Created by

Shakir McDonald

www.thebeekids.com

The B.E.E. Kids Put on Your Thinking H.O.T.S
Copyright © 2013 Shakir McDonald

All rights reserved. No portion of this book may be reproduced, stored in a retrieval system, or transmitted in any form or by any means – electronic, mechanical, photocopy, recording, or any other – except for brief quotations in printed reviews, without the prior permission of the author or publisher.

ISBN-13: 978-0615864631 (B.E.E. Media)
ISBN-10: 0615864635

www.thebeekids.com
info@thebeekids.com

Thank you God for giving me the vision, patience and people necessary to bring this project to life.

Hi there Friend!

I'm the Queen B.E.E. and I'd like to welcome you to The B.E.E. Kids' book series. "B.E.E." is an acronym for Brilliant, Educated and Empowered.
The B.E.E. Kids is a series of books for children ages 5-12 years old. Each book follows the escapades of The B.E.E. Kids plus an ensemble of insects whose habits and beliefs either help them soar to success, or limit their mobility. Together with their guides, the industrious insects cultivate a culture of achievement by challenging 'stinking thinking', learning how to learn and navigating the adventures of academic life.

This book will introduce you to a group of insects called the B.U.G.S, an acronym, that means "Beliefs that Undermine Greatness and Success". The Bugs in this book, like in the real world are a pesky bunch that tend to distract, discourage and deter. The B.U.G.S, consist of Dowdin Yuself (Doubt), Hayden Goode (Negativity), Lil E. Geaux (Pride), Juan Abbey (Self-Acceptance), Gunner Waiyt (Procrastination), and Sheza Frayed (Fear). These characters either embody or defy the Colony Core values of Readiness, Respect, Responsiveness, Responsibility, Receptiveness, and being Reasonable.

📚	**Bee Ready**	having focus and agility in your preparation to perform
❤️	**Bee Responsive**	doing what is necessary to support others in need
🍎	**Bee Responsible**	having the ability to always do what is requested and required
🎧	**Bee Receptive**	being willing to humbly accept others opinions and differences
🔍	**Bee Reflective**	being willing to honestly look inside myself for answers
👄	**Bee Reasonable**	having the flexibility to listen to learn and speak to support

In this book, The B.U.G.S. are tasked with a challenge that requires them to cooperatively and creatively solve a mounting problem by tapping into their "Higher Order Thinking Skills" using the theory of the "Six Thinking Hats". These skills are essential to help students to solve problems that require creativity and critical thinking.

The B.U.G.S will take you along as they each power up their thinking and begin to think in a new fashion and hopefully you'll try on a few hats too!

Sincerely Yours,
The Queen B.E.E.

Educational Overview

Hello Friends,
This story will challenge young readers to "put on your thinking H.O.T.S" or Higher Order Thinking Skills in order to evaluate problems critically, cooperatively, and creatively to effectively power-up their thinking.

With a focus on brain-based learning, this book, will direct you toward a powerful thinking tool, known as Dr. Edward de Bono's Six Thinking Hats. Developed by Dr. Edward DeBono, a physician, author, inventor and consultant, the "Six Thinking Hats" theory, teaches that you must look critically and creatively from six different perspectives to solve a problem or make a complex decision.

This colorful strategy exposes learners to six different styles of thinking and helps them look at a problem from six different perspectives. The Six Thinking Hats approach can be used to address almost any problem-solving activity you might encounter in the classroom or in life. Assigning each thinking style a color serves as a visual cue to help students recognize the critical thinking skill that they are actually using.

White	(facts and figures)
Red	(emotions)
Black	(caution and care)
Yellow	(positive speculation)
Green	(creativity)
Blue	(process, order and control)

Have you ever felt just downright disgusted,
Not because you did wrong but because you were busted?
That Gunner pulled pranks was a well-known fact,
But this time his friends were dragged into the act.
The Bugs find themselves all stuck in detention
For acts that are just too despicable to mention.
Well that is the plight of the bugs on this day,
Seemingly uneventful, until it all went astray.
Sheza, Hayden, Dowdin, Lil, and Juan all round out the band,
But for a boring day in detention, nothing went as they planned.
No one knew this day would be full of adventure and action,
When they are all forced to think in a completely different fashion.

Have you ever felt like these bugs?

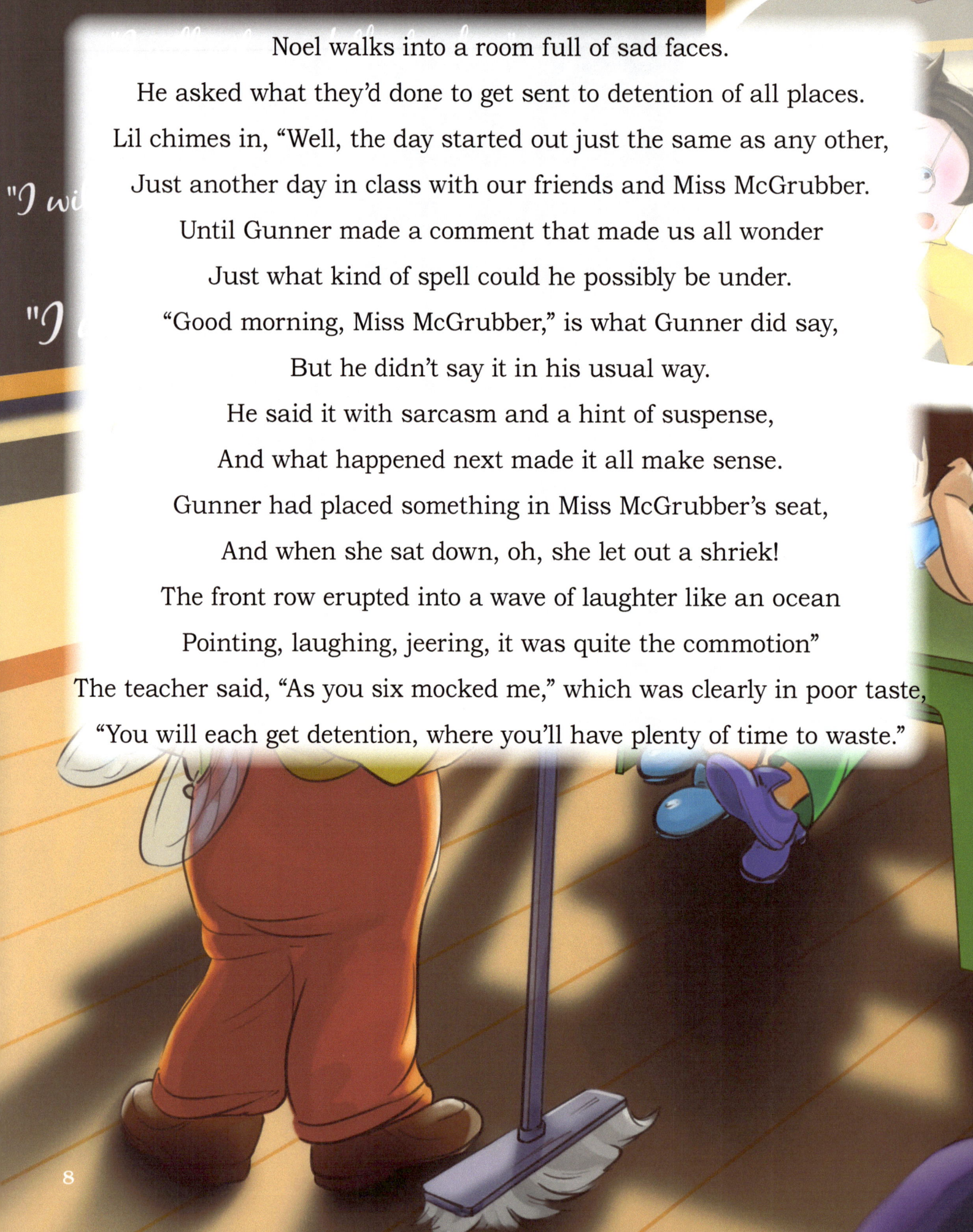

Noel walks into a room full of sad faces.

He asked what they'd done to get sent to detention of all places.

Lil chimes in, "Well, the day started out just the same as any other,

Just another day in class with our friends and Miss McGrubber.

Until Gunner made a comment that made us all wonder

Just what kind of spell could he possibly be under.

"Good morning, Miss McGrubber," is what Gunner did say,

But he didn't say it in his usual way.

He said it with sarcasm and a hint of suspense,

And what happened next made it all make sense.

Gunner had placed something in Miss McGrubber's seat,

And when she sat down, oh, she let out a shriek!

The front row erupted into a wave of laughter like an ocean

Pointing, laughing, jeering, it was quite the commotion"

The teacher said, "As you six mocked me," which was clearly in poor taste,

"You will each get detention, where you'll have plenty of time to waste."

Why do you think it was in poor character to mock the teacher?

Normally, Noel the janitor, always had a lesson,
But this time the smart janitor met them with a question.
Noel says, "I have a problem figuring out a method or course
For items I find when I don't know their source.
These items pile high but I don't want to throw them away
Because I know that the larvae can use them to play.
I know it could be great with a bit of imagination
It just needs some tidying and a tad of organization
Can you six find a solution to help?"
But before he could finish, Noel let out a yelp.
It seems that his lunch had taken a turn too soon,
So Noel ran full speed to the nearest restroom.

What is Noel's problem and what does he ask them to do?

Before Noel ran off, he showed them the site

That was all very wrong that they had to make right.

They peeked in the room that Noel had shown

It was chock full of contents with whereabouts unknown

There were clothes thrown everywhere in complete disarray,

They stood there in shock until it finally went away.

They enter the room to size up the matter

Just where to start was the groups only chatter

Completely overwhelmed by the predicament they were in

No one could agree on just where to begin

There were clothes and books, and it was all quite a mess,

Then all of their eyes fixed on a mysterious chest.

✅ What do you think is in the mysterious chest?

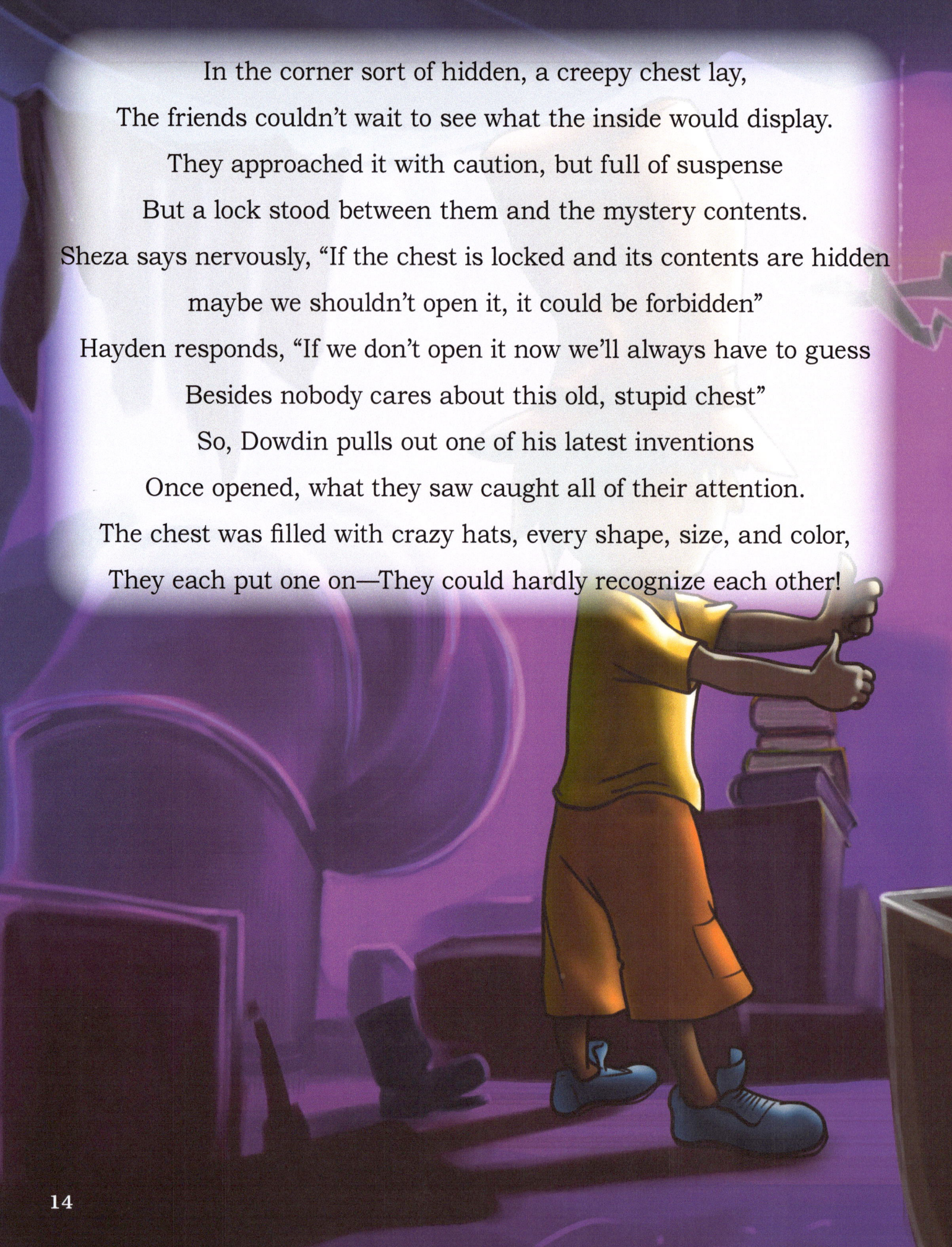

In the corner sort of hidden, a creepy chest lay,
The friends couldn't wait to see what the inside would display.
They approached it with caution, but full of suspense
But a lock stood between them and the mystery contents.
Sheza says nervously, "If the chest is locked and its contents are hidden
maybe we shouldn't open it, it could be forbidden"
Hayden responds, "If we don't open it now we'll always have to guess
Besides nobody cares about this old, stupid chest"
So, Dowdin pulls out one of his latest inventions
Once opened, what they saw caught all of their attention.
The chest was filled with crazy hats, every shape, size, and color,
They each put one on—They could hardly recognize each other!

What do you think will happen when they put on the hats?

First Dowdin goes in and pulls out a white hat for construction,
Then he immediately began to explain his deduction.
Dowdin says, "Let's focus on the data in hand,
Let's see what we can learn and come up with a plan.
Noel needs this closet clean, but with a function,
But there are some gaps in our knowledge at this junction.
Let's see if we can't take account of them in stages,
Like who are these larvae—their likes, dislikes, and ages?
Can we analyze past trends before we mount our attack,
Or should we try to infer from historical data and facts?
We need to sit down and analyze the data we seek,
construction of this magnitude could take us several weeks."

How are having facts and data important when making a decision?

Just as Dowdin was speaking, Lil chimed in,
With a red hat so big you could hardly see her grin.
"Your logic is quite smart but that plan is rather flimsy,
What these larvae need is a place filled with whimsy.
Let's look at this problem using our gut and intuition,
And create them a world in the fairy-tale tradition.
The boys can be knights and the girls damsels of course,
Who ride up to the castle on a beautiful white horse.
I just can't wait to see all of their reactions,
Complete and utter joy—oh, what a delightful attraction!"
But reading their faces, it seemed her idea went south,
Especially when she heard what came out of Hayden's mouth.

Why are emotions and feelings important when making a decision?

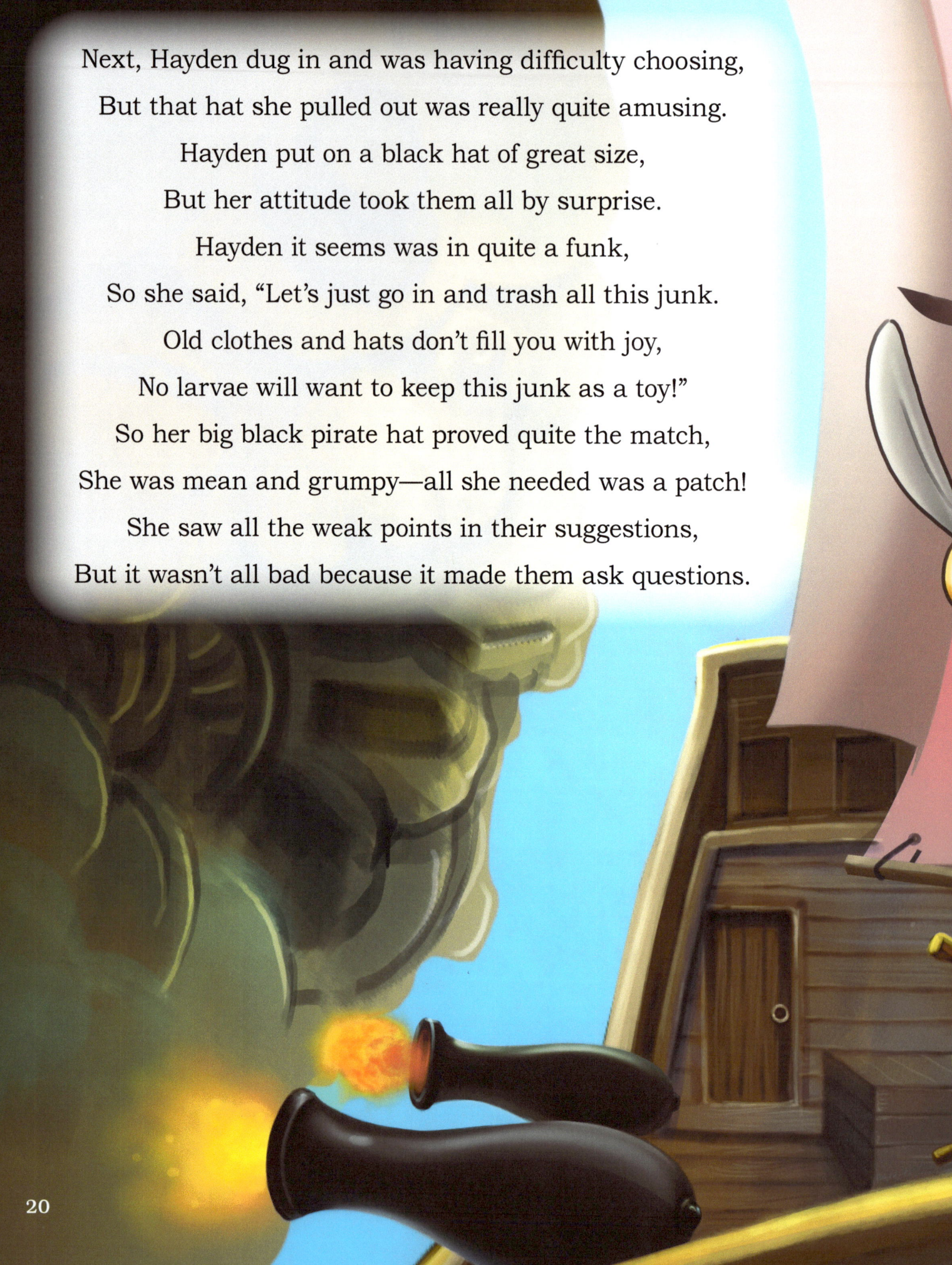

Next, Hayden dug in and was having difficulty choosing,

But that hat she pulled out was really quite amusing.

Hayden put on a black hat of great size,

But her attitude took them all by surprise.

Hayden it seems was in quite a funk,

So she said, "Let's just go in and trash all this junk.

Old clothes and hats don't fill you with joy,

No larvae will want to keep this junk as a toy!"

So her big black pirate hat proved quite the match,

She was mean and grumpy—all she needed was a patch!

She saw all the weak points in their suggestions,

But it wasn't all bad because it made them ask questions.

Are negative viewpoints and opinions helpful when solving a problem?

They sat there stuck, no solution in sight,
Until Sheza says, putting on her hat, "Maybe you're all right."
Sheza put on a hat that made everyone smile,
because for what it had in color it truly lacked in style.
Wearing a bright-yellow hat with a headlight for sight,
Sheza says, "Let's look at this in a more positive light.
You all offered ideas that were really quite keen,
But maybe we can explore them more in depth while we clean.
I like Dowdin's planning and Lil's ideas shouldn't be excused,
But, like Hayden says, we should discard what can't be reused.
Let's try and use it all and throw away what can't be reprised,
But I call first dibs on this hat, if that's okay with you guys!"

What positive points did Sheza see in the other suggestions?

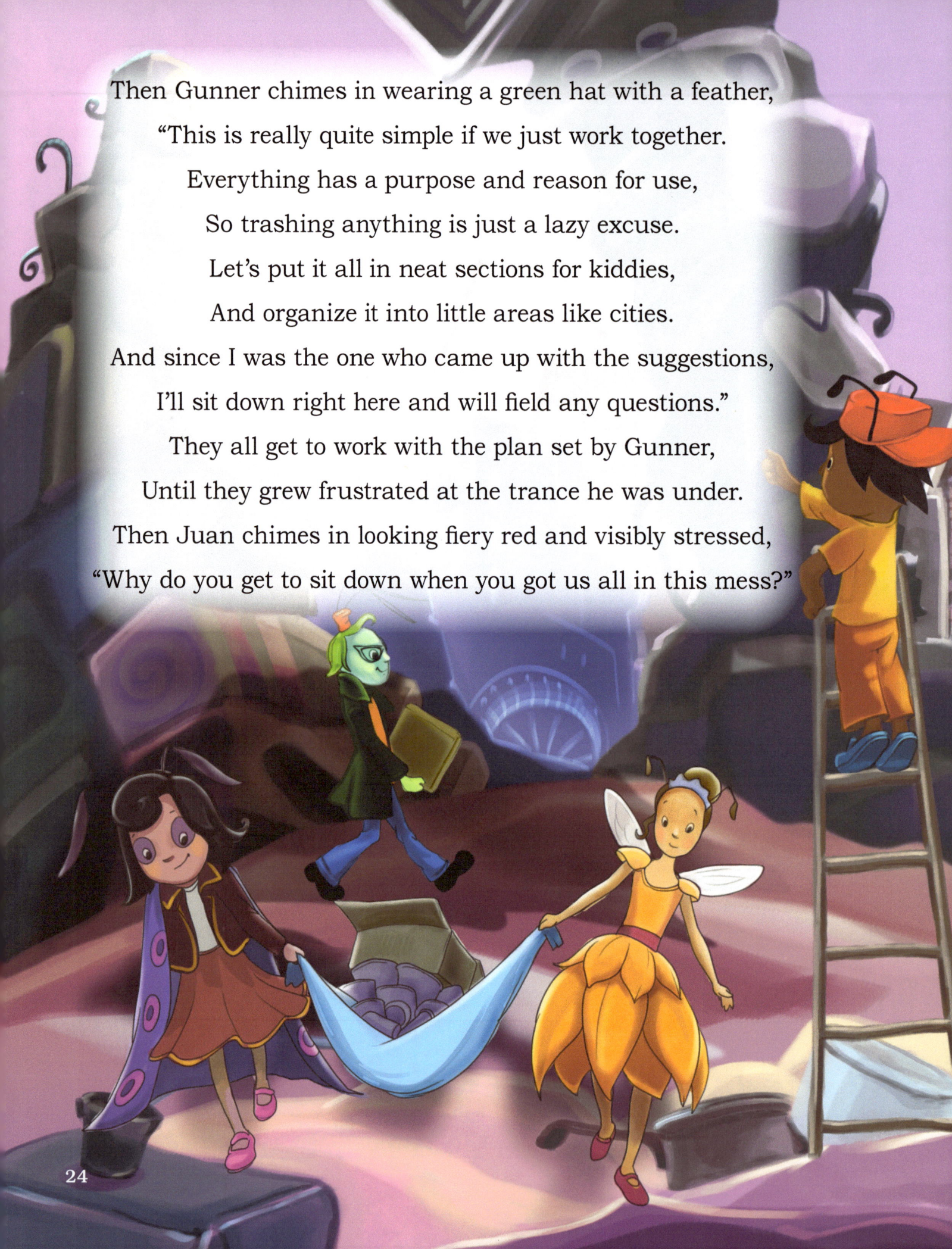

Then Gunner chimes in wearing a green hat with a feather,
"This is really quite simple if we just work together.
Everything has a purpose and reason for use,
So trashing anything is just a lazy excuse.
Let's put it all in neat sections for kiddies,
And organize it into little areas like cities.
And since I was the one who came up with the suggestions,
I'll sit down right here and will field any questions."
They all get to work with the plan set by Gunner,
Until they grew frustrated at the trance he was under.
Then Juan chimes in looking fiery red and visibly stressed,
"Why do you get to sit down when you got us all in this mess?"

How was Gunner suggesting new ideas helpful?

They all had been duped and no one knew what really happened,

So Juan digs in the crate and pulls out the hat of a police captain.

Juan looked like a model of strength and security,

And with that blue hat, they all respected his authority.

Juan says, "using Gunner's idea, we can take care of a chunk,

While Hayden can be responsible for trashing the junk.

Me, Gunner and Dowdin can do the transporting,

While Sheza and Lil can be in charge of the sorting.

Us boys can bring all the stuff over there like a team,

While the girls sort them by gender, size and theme."

With a cooperative plan in action, it was really quite fun,

So by the time they looked up they were already done.

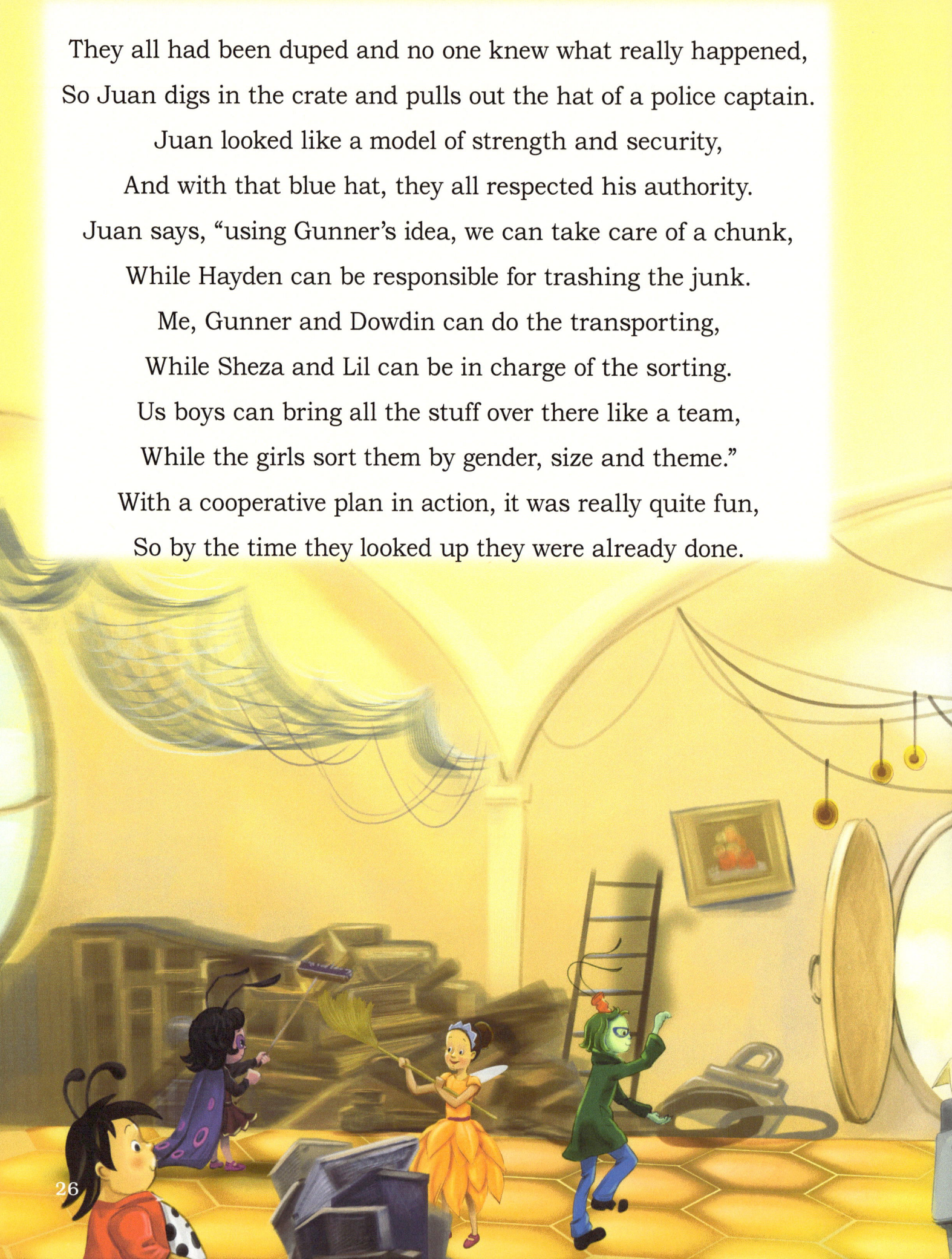

How did Juan organize the group's thinking?

Noel came back and was really quite impressed,
That they'd come up with these ideas by using the hats in the chest.
He said that he watched the whole time and never really went away,
Hayden got mad and said, "So you just got us to do your job for the day!"
Noel sprays his BUGS spray and says, "perhaps now you'll understand,
With that white hat, Dowdin was able to analyze and plan.
Each hat controlled the way that your thinking did go,
And while the yellow was quite positive, the red allowed emotion to flow.
Black allowed you to see the flaws and the areas you needed to address,
While green gave a creative solution, blue was able to control the process."
He explained to them the lesson that he hoped they had learned,
And the wealth of thinking strategies they'd actually earned.

How did each hat change their thinking?

Noel went on to further explain,

That they should use their six thinking hats before reacting again.

That when people's feelings get hurt, pranks are no longer funny,

And that they attract less bees with vinegar and more if they use honey.

To remember the lessons they learned with the hats,

That before they make a decision they should first consider the facts,

Use their gut, think positively, but don't forget to consider the errors,

Brainstorm, come up with a creative solution to manage the process together.

Noel sent them back to class where they'd finally be put to the test,

Before they left he said, "You six—I have one final request.

What do you think Noel is going to ask them to do?

Noel says, "Think of something you can do for your teacher
to make the situation right,
To show her that you now know better and that you understand her plight."
They decide to make this decision using their new skills, starting from scratch,
When Dowdin says, "Let's solve this problem by first considering the facts."
Lil says, "But let's use our intuition and consider her feelings first,
When Sheza says, "Well, on the bright side, we can't make the situation worse."
So Hayden says, "But if this goes wrong, it could blow up in our faces,"
Sheza says, "Yeah, but it could also put us back in her good graces."
Gunner says, "Since I got us into this, allow me to make a suggestion,
Then Juan says, "and we can apologize in front of the class."
Then Juan says, "and we can clean the room in question."
Now armed with a plan they went to their class to seal their solemn fate,
To make amends for what they'd done; before it was too late.

✓ How did they use the 6 thinking hats to help them solve this problem?

They walked into class and everything stopped,

All eyes were on them and you could hear a pin drop.

In a single-file line they made their way to the front,

And they had more attention than any of them could ever want.

So they cleared their throats and began to address their class and Miss McGrubber,

They knew they had to make it right one way or another.

Gunner stepped up and confidently spoke,

"I'm truly sorry for the disruption I created with my joke.

I was inconsiderate and didn't think my decision through,

And it led to a punishment for my friends here too."

"Noel taught us that we should think six ways before taking any single action,

But thanks to Noel we're all thinking in an entirely different fashion."

Why do you think that apologizing to their teacher was important?

Check Points 1
Have you ever felt like these Bugs?

Check Points 2
Do you think the friends should have gotten in trouble for laughing?

Check Points 3
What does Noel need them to do in the room?

Check Points 4
What do you think is in the mysterious chest?

Check Points 5
What do you think is happening to them when they put on the hats?

Check Points 6
Do you think having facts and data are important when making a decision?

Check Points 7
Do you think having emotions and feelings are important when making a decision?

Check Points 8
Do you think Hayden's negative judgements or opinions were helpful?

Check Points 9
What positive points did Sheza see in the other suggestions?

Check Points 10
Do you think Gunner suggesting new ideas was helpful?

Check Points 11
How did Juan organize the groups thinking?

Check Points 12
How did each hat change their thinking?

Check Points 13
Do you think that the Bugs should have to apologize for their actions?

Check Points 14
How were the thinking hats, helpful in helping them solve this problem?

Check Points 15
Can you identify all six thinking hats?

Educational Recap

The magical hats in the chest caused the B.U.G.S to see each other and their problem differently. The hats helped them to learn to understand each other and work together in spite of their initial differences. Next time you need help to solve a problem, put on your thinking H.O.T.S. (Higher Order Thinking Skills)

* Remember, the individual Bugs and how each hat gave them each a unique point of view to help them solve the problem together.

Dowdin Yuself
White Hat (Information)

Ask Yourself: What are the facts?

Lil E. Geaux
Red Hat (Feelings)

Ask Yourself: What do I feel about this?

Hayden Goode
Black Hat (Judgment)

Ask Yourself: What is wrong with this?

Sheza Frayed
Yellow Hat (Benefits)

Ask Yourself: What are the good points?

Gunner Wayte
Green Hat (Creativity)

Ask Yourself: What new ideas are possible?

Juan Abbey
Blue Hat (Thinking)

Ask Yourself: What thinking is needed?

About the Author

Shakir McDonald, also known as The Queen B.E.E., is a dedicated wife, mother, author, entrepreneur, mentor, youth advocate, motivational speaker and radio host.

A bright student that struggled discovering her own smarts, Shakir became a teacher to find innovative ways to help students like herself build confidence and academic competency. Shakir found solace in the classroom but found that students needed more support than the time spent in class could afford.

Inspired by a mission to help reveal the brilliance in children through education and empower students with lifelong tools for success, confidence, and a renewed fascination for learning, Shakir founded The Brilliant, Educated, and Empowered (B.E.E.) Academy.
The B.E.E. Academy™ is an innovative resource, serving a multitude of children through tutoring, after-school programs, classes and camps.

Shakir developed the "The B.E.E. Kids" book series to equip, entertain and educate children, parents and educators about the "B.E.E. Way" – a proven model of cultivating academic achievement for school age youth. This methodology is fused into The B.E.E. Kids' books as exciting characters, story lines and themes that whisk kids away on adventures in fun and fundamentals.

www.ingramcontent.com/pod-product-compliance
Lightning Source LLC
LaVergne TN
LVHW072127070426
835512LV00002B/30